1920s FASHION DESIGN

MODEDESIGN DER ZWANZIGER JAHRE
DISEÑOS DE LA MODA EN LOS AÑOS 1920
FASHION DESIGN DEGLI ANNI VENTI
LA MODE DES ANNÉES 1920

1920s FASHION DESIGN

MODEDESIGN DER ZWANZIGER JAHRE
DISEÑOS DE LA MODA EN LOS AÑOS 1920
FASHION DESIGN DEGLI ANNI VENTI
LA MODE DES ANNÉES 1920

P

THE PEPIN PRESS

The Pepin Press Design Series

GRAPHIC ORNAMENTS 1900

CORNER & BORDER DESIGNS 1900

ORNAMENTAL DESIGN 1850

DECORATED PAPER DESIGNS 1800

ARCHITECTURE DRAWINGS

DESIGNS OF NATURE

4000 MONOGRAMS

A PICTORIAL HISTORY OF COSTUME

STRUCTURAL PACKAGE DESIGN

INDONESIAN ORNAMENTAL DESIGN

1930S COMMERCIAL ART

FASHION DESIGN 1850-1895

HATS

More titles in preparation

Copyright for this edition © 1998 The Pepin Press B/V

Copyright introduction '1920s Fashion Design' © 1998 The Pepin Press B/V

First published in 1998 by The Pepin Press

Edited and produced by Joost Hölscher
Cover by Dorine van den Beukel

Introduction by Joost Hölscher; copy-editing Andrew May
Translations: Sebastian Viebahn (German); LocTeam (Spanish);
Anne Loescher (French); Luciano Borelli (Italian)

ISBN 90 5496 053 1

The Pepin Press
POB 10349
1001 EH Amsterdam
The Netherlands
Tel (+) 31 20 4202021
Fax (+) 31 20 4201152
mail@pepinpress.com

Printed in Singapore

Fashion Design in the 1920s

This Pepin Press book contains a large collection of fashion drawings dating from 1920 to 1930. As with other volumes in this series, this book is not intended to provide a complete survey of fashion in the twenties, but to offer a selection of high-quality reproductions as reference material and a source of inspiration for designers and anyone who is interested in the fashions of the first decade of the interbellum.

When textiles rationing was lifted after the First World War, the frugality, functionality and common sense of wartime dress had become irrevocably entrenched. The raising of hemlines above the ankle for the first time in recorded history, and the abandoning of the constrictive and unwholesome wasp waist, was so much appreciated by women that fashion designers and clothing manufacturers were entirely unsuccessful in trying to restore pre-war elegance and opulence. Simplicity remained fashionable for men as well as for women: lounge suits replaced frock-coats; soft trilbies and Homburgs ousted the silk top-hat; shirt collars became lower and softer, and dinner-jackets increasingly took over from white tie and tails.

The trend of shrugging off Victorian restrictions and exploring new social activities open to women which had set in even before the war was enormously boosted by the war. Thousands of women had been mobilised to keep the economy running while the men were fighting. Traditionally male professions like office clerk were all taken over by women, and the female conquest of the relatively new typewriter was consolidated during the war. Bicycling became a popular mode of transport. All this called for functional, comfortable clothes.

Emancipation, however, was quite a new thing. It has been suggested that women did not yet feel entirely comfortable with this, which seems to be reflected in fashion. The general feeling at the time was such that women had to appear less feminine in order to be as successful as men. This resulted in a rather androgynous, boyish look, that played down all feminine aspects of the physique: breasts were flattened; the waist was not accentuated; hips were hidden under an extremely low waistline and hair was cut short.

In painting and architecture, on the other hand, which had both very little to do with women's liberation, curved forms were also being supplanted by straight lines, suggesting movement, simplicity and new beginnings. This parallel implies a wider and deeper origin for the transformation of couture than mere male competition.

Voluptuousness was associated with decadence, and any trace of roundedness was frowned upon as a sign of uncontrolled eating habits. The newly exposed legs, ideally, were quite thin. In some more puritanical countries this unhindered view of female ankles caused public indignation and occasionally even legal sanctions, but the old moralities, which had been responsible for perpetuating the slaughter on the western front, were definitely losing their sway.

High fashion reluctantly adapted to all these changes and, for the first time ever, responded to youthful, middle-class demand. Designers could no longer authoritatively decree what was à la mode without regard for popular demand. Fashion had started to become liberated and democratic.

Modedesign der zwanziger Jahre

Dieses Pepin Press-Buch enthält eine umfangreiche Sammlung von Modezeichnungen aus der Zeit von 1920 bis 1930. Wie die anderen Bände dieser Serie will auch dieses Buch keinen vollständigen Überblick über die Mode der zwanziger Jahre geben, sondern eine Auswahl hochwertiger Reproduktionen als Referenzmaterial und Inspirationsquelle für Designer und alle die anbieten, die sich für das Gesicht des ersten Jahrzehnts in der Zeit zwischen den Weltkriegen interessieren.

Es war nur logisch, dass sich die Schlichtheit, Funktionalität und Rationalität der Kleidung aus der Kriegszeit auch nach der Aufhebung der Textilienrationierung nach Ende des Ersten Weltkriegs hielt. Die erstmals seit Menschengedenken kürzer als auf Knöchellänge getragenen Röcke und der Abschied von der einengenden und ungesunden Wespentaille fanden so grossen Anklang bei den Frauen, dass Modedesigner und Kleidungshersteller in ihren Versuchen, Eleganz und Opulenz der Vorkriegszeiten wiederaufleben zu lassen, nicht den geringsten Erfolg hatten.

Einfachheit blieb Mode, sowohl für Herren als auch für Damen. Strassenanzüge ersetzten Gehröcke, weiche Trilbies und Homburgs verdrängten den Seidenzylinder, die Hemdkragen wurden schmaler und weicher, und der Smoking setzte sich zunehmend gegen weisse Krawatte und Frack durch.

Schon vor Kriegsbeginn hatten die Frauen begonnen, die Beschränkungen des Viktorianischen Zeitalters abzuschütteln und neue gesellschaftliche Tätigkeitsfelder zu erkunden, die ihnen offenstanden; dieser Trend wurde durch den Krieg enorm forciert. Hundertausende Frauen wurden mobilisiert, um die Wirtschaft in Gang zu halten, während die Männer an der Front kämpften. Alle traditionell männlichen Berufe, wie beispielsweise Büroangestellter, wurden von Frauen übernommen, und während des Krieges verfestigte sich die weibliche Vorherrschaft über die noch nicht sehr lange eingeführte Schreibmaschine. Radfahren wurde zu einer populären Fortbewegungsart. All dies verlangte nach funktionaler, bequemer Kleidung.

Die Emanzipation war jedoch noch etwas Neues. Es wird sogar behauptet, dass sich viele Frauen damals in dieser Rolle noch nicht so wohl fühlten, was sich offenbar in der Mode niederschlug. Allgemein empfand man damals anscheinend, dass Frauen weniger feminin aussehen mussten, wenn sie ebenso erfolgreich sein wollten wie Männer; das führte zu einem recht androgynen, knabenhaften Look mit einem Understatement aller femininen Aspekte des Körpers. Man vermied die Betonung der Taille, hielt die Brustpartie flach, kaschierte die Hüften durch eine extrem niedrige Gürtellinie und trug das Haar kurz.

Wenngleich Malerei und Architektur eigentlich nichts mit Frauenemanzipation zu tun hatten, wurden auch hier Kurven von geraden Linien verdrängt, die Bewegung, Einfachheit und Neubeginn suggerierten. Dies weist darauf hin, dass es sich hier nicht lediglich um einen banalen Wettkampf zwischen den Geschlechtern handelte. Üppigkeit wurde mit Dekadenz assoziiert, und die kleinste Spur von Rundlichkeit missbilligend als Zeichen unkontrollierten Essens betrachtet. So waren die erstmals entblössten Beine im Idealfall relativ dünn. Sie gaben in einigen eher puritanischen Ländern Anlass zu öffentlichem Ärgernis und in Einzelfällen sogar zu gesetzlichen Sanktionen. Die alten Moralvorstellungen aber, die für das anhaltende Kriegsgemetzel an der Westfront verantwortlich gewesen waren, hatten definitiv ihren Einfluss verloren.

Die Haute Couture passte sich diesen Veränderungen widerstrebend an und wurde damit zum ersten Mal von der Nachfrage der jungen Mittelschicht bestimmt. Modeschöpfer konnten nicht länger autoritär diktieren, was à la mode war, ohne auf die Bedürfnisse der Allgemeinheit zu achten. Die Mode begann freier und demokratischer zu werden.

Modèles de mode dans les années 1920

Cet ouvrage des éditions Pepin Press regroupe une large collection de croquis de mode des années 1920 à 1930. Comme pour les autres volumes de cette série, l'intention de ce livre n'est pas de fournir une étude exhaustive de la mode dans les années 1920, mais de proposer une sélection de reproductions de haute qualité comme un matriel de référence et une source d'inspiration pour les créateurs et tous ceux intéressés par la mode de cette première décade de l'entre-deux guerres.

Quand le rationnement des textiles fut soulevé après la première guerre mondiale, il était évident que la frugalité, le caractère fonctionnel et le bon sens du costume du temps de guerre demeurent. Le racourcissement des ourlets au-dessus de la cheville, enregistré pour la première fois dans l'histoire, et l'abandon de la taille de guêpe, contraignante et nocive pour la santé, étaient tellement appréciés des femmes que les créateurs de mode restaient totalement sans succès dans leur effort de restaurer l'élégance et l'opulence d'avant la guerre. Pour les hommes comme pour les femmes, la simplicité demeurait la mode. Les complets remplaçaient les redingotes, les chapeaux mous et les feutres évinçaient le haut-de-forme de soie, les cols de chemises devinrent plus souples et moins hauts et les smokings supplantaient de plus en plus le noeud papillon blanc et les queues de pie.

La tendance à ignorer les restrictions Victoriennes et l'exploration de nouvelles activités sociales ouvertes aux femmes, déjà amorcée avant la guerre, fut énormément renforcée par la guerre. Des milliers de femmes furent mobilisées pour continuer à maintenir l'économie en activité pendant que les hommes combattaient sur le front. Les professions traditionnellement masculines, comme employé de bureau étaient toutes occupées par des femmes, et la conquête féminine de la relativement nouvelle machine à écrire fut consolidée pendant la guerre. La bicyclette devint un moyen de transport populaire. Tout ceci nécéssitait des vêtements fonctionnels et confortables. Cependant, l'émancipation était une notion assez neuve et il a été suggéré que les femmes ne se sentaient pas encore complètement à l'aise avec celle-ci; ce qui semblait se ressentir dans la mode. Le sentiment général de l'époque a été tel qu'afin de réussir autant que les hommes, les femmes devaient afficher une apparence moins féminine, ce qui par conséquence entraîna une allure plutôt androgyne et garçonnière, minimisant tous les aspects féminins du physique. La poitrine était aplatie, la taille n'était pas accentuée, les hanches étaient dissimulées sous une taille extrêmement basse, et les cheveux étaient coupés courts.

Bien que la peinture et l'architecture n'aient pas de liens avec la libration des femmes, les formes arrondies y furent également supplantées par des lignes droites, suggérant le mouvement, la simplicité et les nouveaux débuts. Cela indique qu'il s'agitait ici d'un tendance plus profonde qu'une simple lutte des sexes.

La volupté était associée avec la décadence, et toute trace de rondeur était désapprouvée et vue comme un signe d'habitudes alimentaires incontrôlées. Les jambes récemment dénudées, ce qui causait dans certains pays plus puritains l'indignation publique et occasionnellement des sanctions légales, étaient idéalement très minces. Les vieilles valeurs morales qui avaient été responsables du maintien des massacres sur le front ouest avaient sans aucun doute perdu leur emprise.

La haute couture s'est adaptée à regret à ces changements et pour la première fois, prouva quelle était contrôlée par la demande de la jeune classe moyenne. Les créateurs ne pouvaient plus arbitrairement déclarer ce qui constituait la mode sans prendre en considération les exigences populaires. La mode avait commencée être libre et démocratique.

Il design di moda negli anni Venti

Questo libro, edito dalla Pepin Press, contiene una vasta collezione di disegni di moda datati dal 1920 al 1930. Come anche per altri volumi di questa serie lo scopo di questo libro non è fornire una panoramica completa della moda degli anni venti ma di presentare una selezione di riproduzioni di alta qualità che serva sia come materiale di riferimento che come spunto per stilisti ed anche per chiunque abbia interesse ad approfondire questa storica decade compresa tra i due conflitti mondiali.

Quando, dopo la prima guerra mondiale, il razionamento dei tessuti fu tolto, la frugalità, la funzionalità ed il comune senso del vestire tipico del periodo di guerra erano ormai caratteristiche destinate a restare presenti. Per la prima volta nella storia si assistette all'innalzamento degli orli oltre la linea del ginocchio e l'abbandono della costrittiva e malsana "vitino di vespa". Questo piacque talmente alle donne che i designers e i produttori che tentarono un ritorno all'eleganza e all'opulenza ante-guerra, non ebbero più alcun successo. La semplicità restò di moda, sia per gli uomini che per le donne. Gli abiti da passeggio presero il posto delle giacche alla finanziera, i cappelli flosci di feltro e gli Homburg sostituirono i cilindri, i colletti delle camice divennero più bassi e morbidi e le giacche da pranzo soppiantarono lentamente le cravatte e le marsine bianche.

La moda di contravvenire le restrizioni vittoriane e di esplorare nuove attività sociali per le donne, era un atteggiamento già iniziato prima del conflitto mondiale ed ebbe un enorme sviluppo proprio grazie alla guerra. Migliaia di donne vennero mobilitate affinché l'economia continuasse a funzionare mentre gli uomini conbattevano al fronte. Le professioni tipicamente maschili, come ad esempio nel settore impiegatizio, vennero svolte da donne e la conquista femminile, della relativamente nuova macchina da scrivere si consolidò durante la guerra. Anche l'utilizzo della bicicletta come mezzo di trasporto ebbe un forte incremento e tutte queste attività richiedevano abiti funzionali e comodi.

L'emancipazione era tuttavia una novità e si ritiene che le donne non si trovassero completamente a proprio agio in questo ruolo con conseguenze anche dal punto di vista della moda. Generalmente si pensava che per essere altrettando di successo quanto gli uomini si dovesse apparire meno femminili preferendo un look un po' androgeno, da maschietto, eliminando ogni aspetto fisico femminile come i seni spianati, la vita non accentuata, i fianchi nascosti da linee della vita basse e un taglio di capelli corto.

Anche nella pittura e nella scultura, nonostante queste poco avessero a che fare con la liberazione delle donne, le forme tonde vennero sostituite da linee rette che solo suggerivano il movimento, la semplicità e nuovi orizzonti.

La voluttà veniva associata alla dedadenza e ogni forma di rotondità veniva additata quale abitudine alimentare incontrollata. Le gambe, che venivano ora messe in mostra, oltre a provocare in alcuni paesi più puritani l'indignazione pubblica e occasionalmente addirittura sanzioni, venivano considerate ideali quando queste fossero sottili. La vecchia moralità, responsabile dei massacri del fronte occidentale, perse cosí definitivamente la sua influenza.

L'alta, moda da parte sua, faticò ad adeguarsi a questi cambiamenti e, per la prima volta, si trovò ad essere influenzata da una domanda più giovanile e proveniente dalla classe media. Gli stilisti non poterono più dettare in modo autoritario quale fosse la moda senza tener conto della domanda popolare e anche la moda iniziò così ad essere più libera e democratica.

El diseño de la moda en los años veinte

Este libro de Pepin Press contiene un gran número de diseños de moda que datan de la década de los años veinte. Al igual que en los otros volúmenes de esta serie, la intención de este libro no es dar una visión general de la moda de los años veinte, sino ofrecer una selección de reproducciones de alta calidad como material de referencia y como fuente de inspiración para diseñadores o para cualquier persona que esté interesada en la imagen de la primera década del periodo de entreguerras.

Cuando el racionamiento de los tejidos fue suprimido tras la Primera Guerra Mundial, la frugalidad, funcionalidad y sentido común de la forma de vestir durante la guerra permanecieron. Las mujeres agradecieron tanto que el bajo de la falda subiera por primera vez en la historia por encima de los tobillos y que se abandonara la constrictiva e incómoda moda de lucir una cintura de avispa, que los diseñadores y los fabricantes de ropa fracasaron totalmente al intentar reimplantar la opulencia y elegancia de antes de la guerra. Tanto para los hombres como para las mujeres, la simplicidad en el vestir siguió estando de moda. Los trajes de calle reemplazaron las levitas y los sombreros flexibles, y los *Homburgs* desbancaron a los sombreros de copa de seda. Los cuellos de las camisas se hicieron más bajos y suaves y poco a poco los esmóquines ganaron terreno a la corbata blanca y a los faldones.

La tendencia a rebelarse contra las restricciones victorianas y a explorar nuevas actividades sociales abiertas a las mujeres, que ya se había asentado antes de la guerra, aumentó enormemente debido a ésta. Miles de mujeres habían sido movilizadas para mantener la economía mientras los hombres luchaban en el frente. Las profesiones tradicionalmente masculinas, como la de funcionario, fueron ocupadas por mujeres y la conquista femenina de la relativamente nueva máquina de escribir se consolidó durante la guerra. La bicicleta se convirtió en un medio de transporte muy popular que requería una forma de vestir funcional y cómoda. La emancipación, no obstante, era algo muy nuevo, y se ha sugerido que las mujeres no se sentían del todo cómodas con respecto a este tema, lo que aparece reflejado en la moda. Se dice que en esta época la opinión general era que para tener tanto éxito como los hombres, las mujeres tenían que mostrarse menos femeninas, dar una imagen algo andrógina y masculina y disimular los aspectos femeninos de su físico. Los pechos se ocultaban, la cintura no se acentuaba, las caderas se escondían con un talle muy bajo y el pelo se llevaba corto.

Aunque la pintura y la arquitectura no tienen nada que ver con la liberación de la mujer, las formas curvas también se suplantaban por líneas rectas, que sugerían movimiento, simplicidad y nuevos principios. Lo que indica una movida más profunda que simplemente una lucha entre los sexos.

La voluptuosidad se asociaba con la decadencia y cualquier trazo de redondez era reprobado como símbolo de malos hábitos de alimentación. Las piernas, que se mostraban descubiertas y que en algunos países puritanos causaban indignación pública, incluso sanciones legales, debían ser más bien delgadas. La vieja moral, que había sido la responsable de que continuara la matanza en el frente occidental, había perdido su poder de forma definitiva.

La alta costura se adaptó con cierto reparo a todos estos cambios y, por primera vez, se demostró que estaba controlada por las demandas de los jóvenes de clase media. Los diseñadores ya no pudieron imponer la moda sin tener en cuenta las preferencias del público. La moda había empezado a liberarse y a democratizarse.

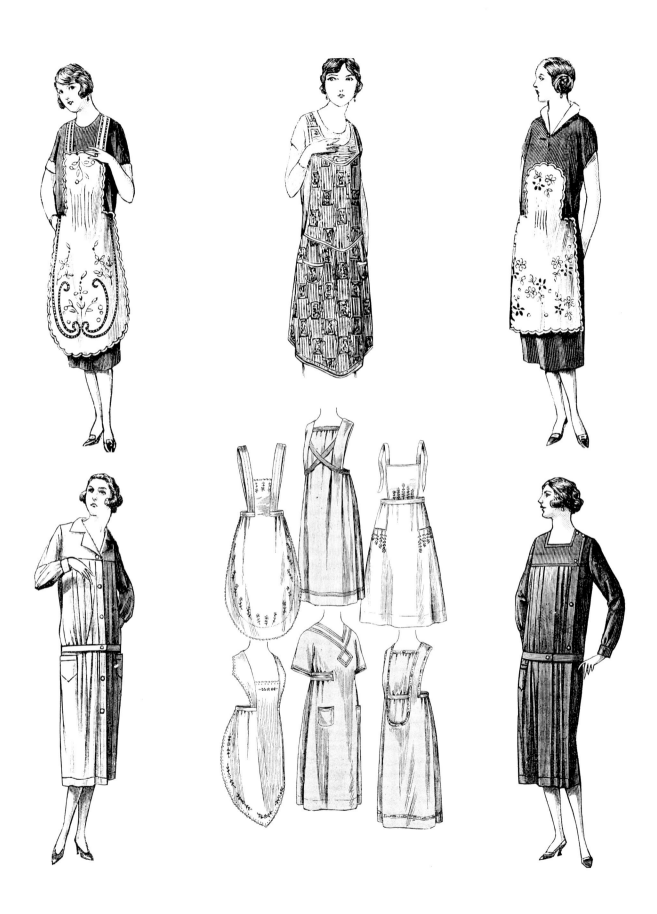

34

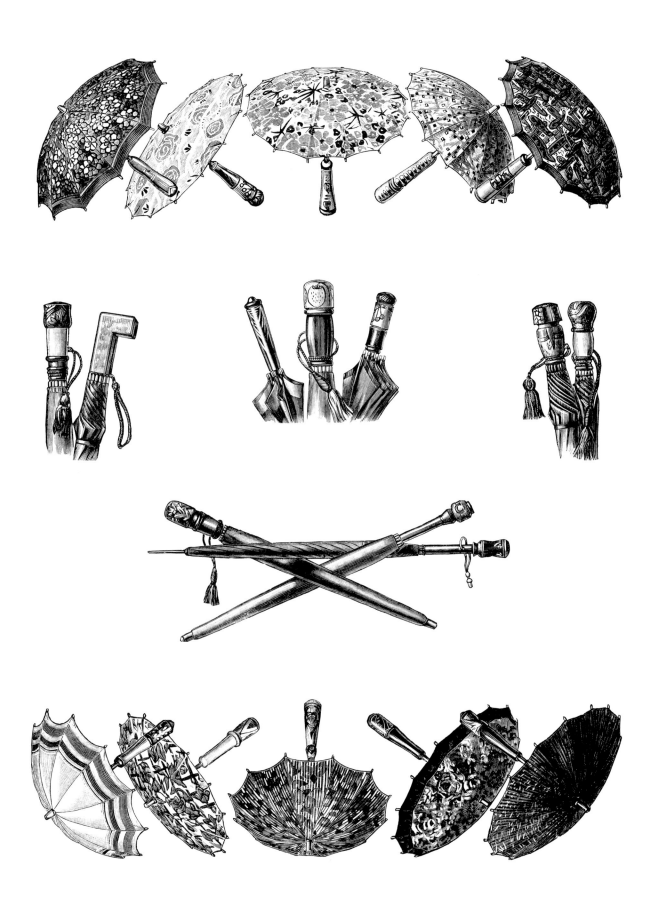

K. 19611   K. 19612

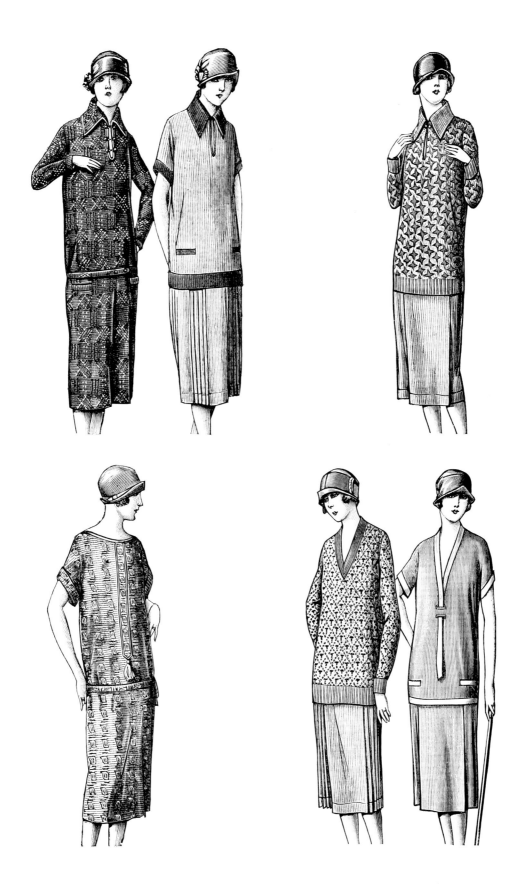

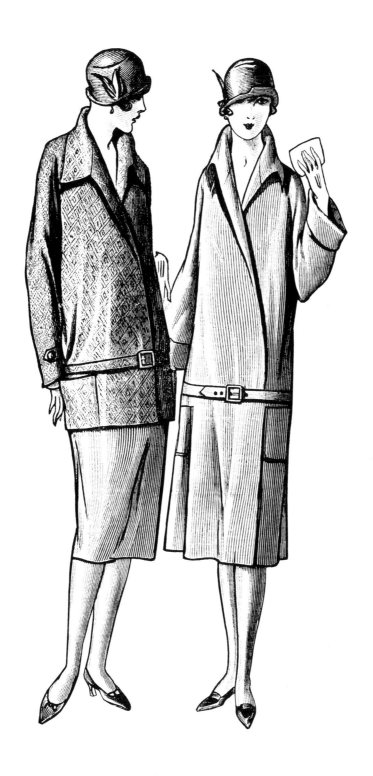

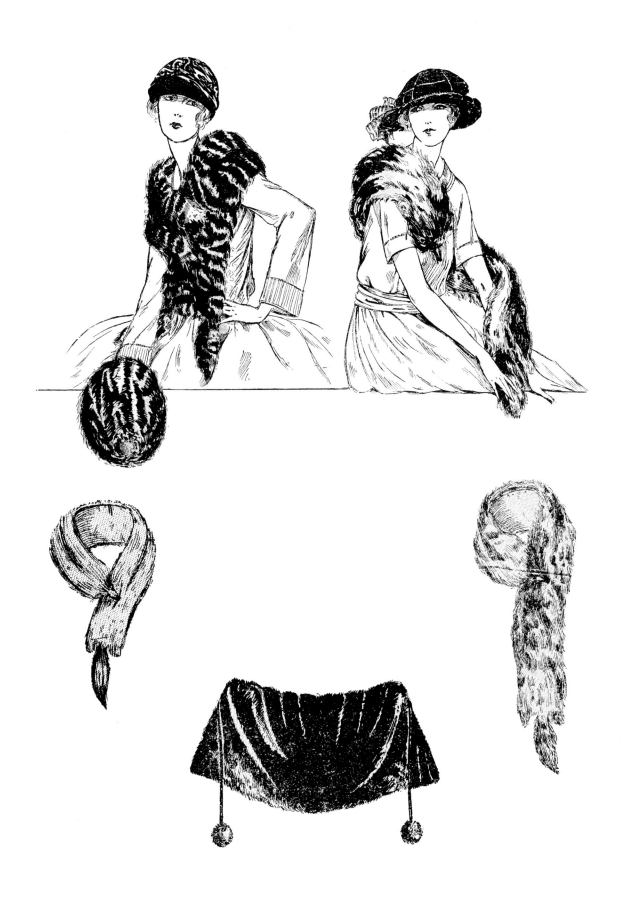

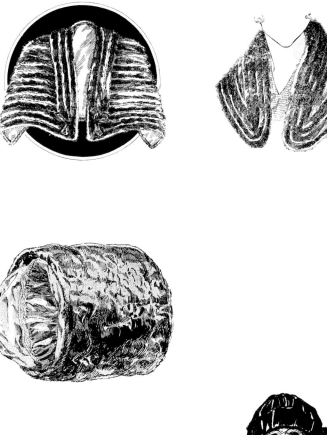

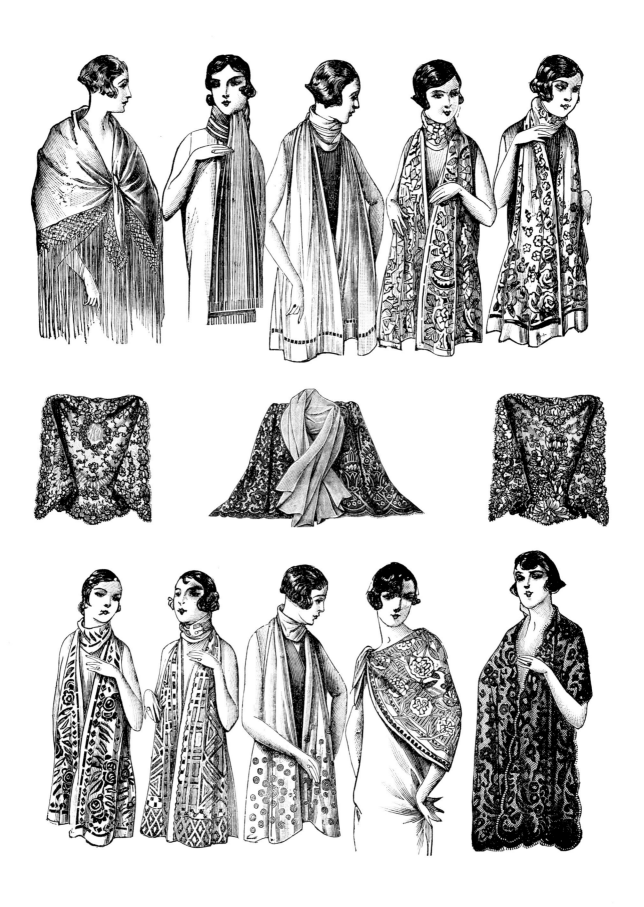

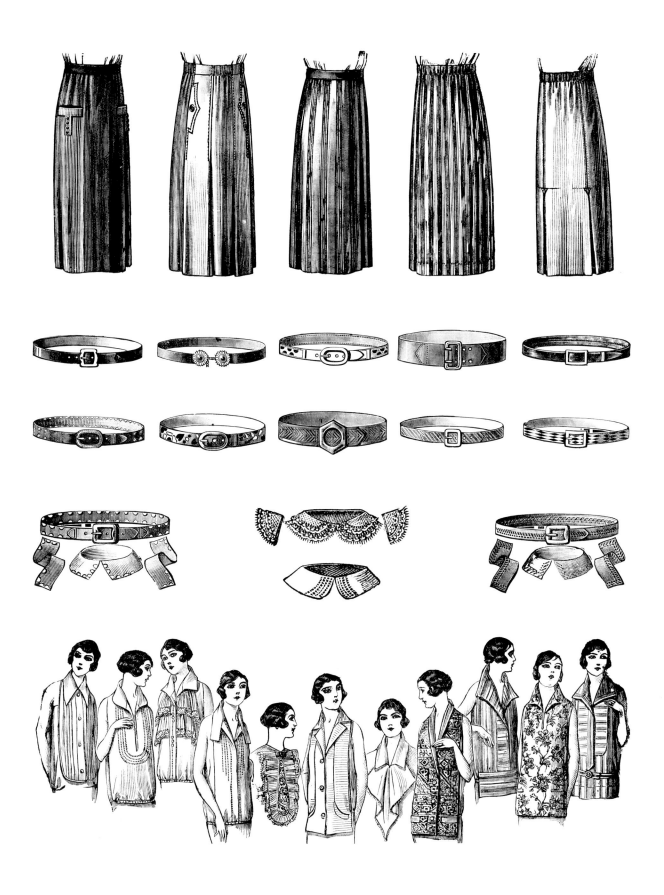

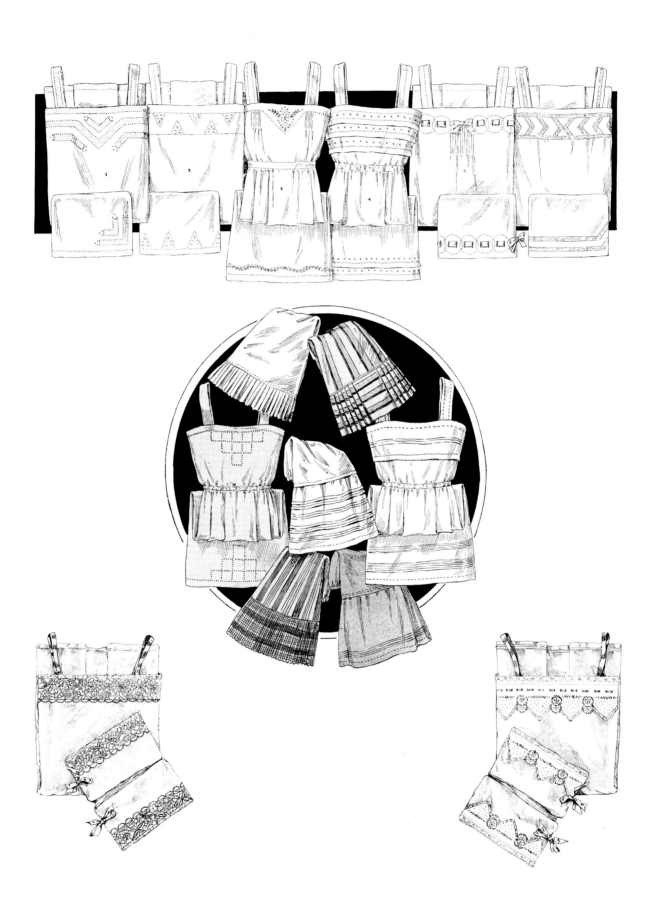

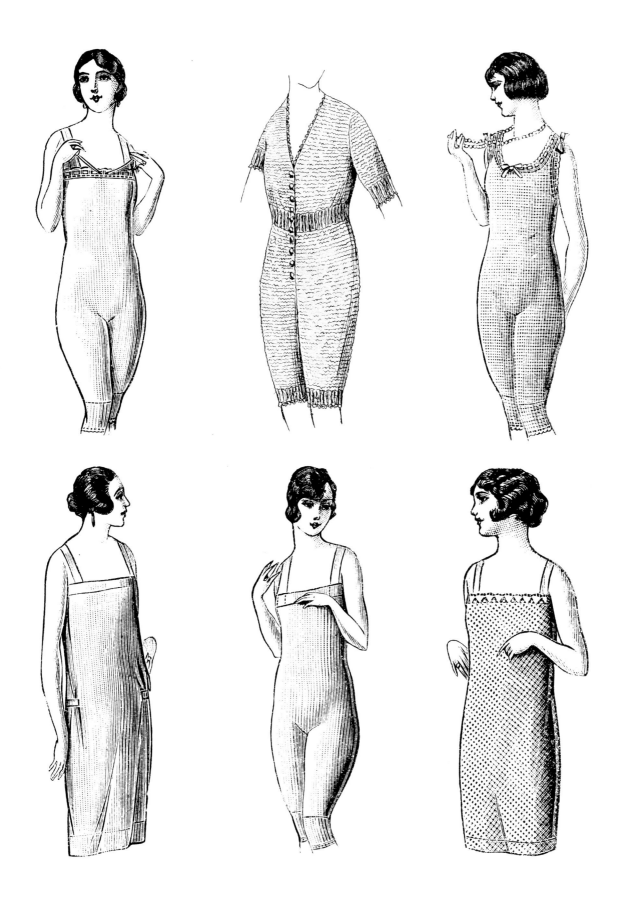

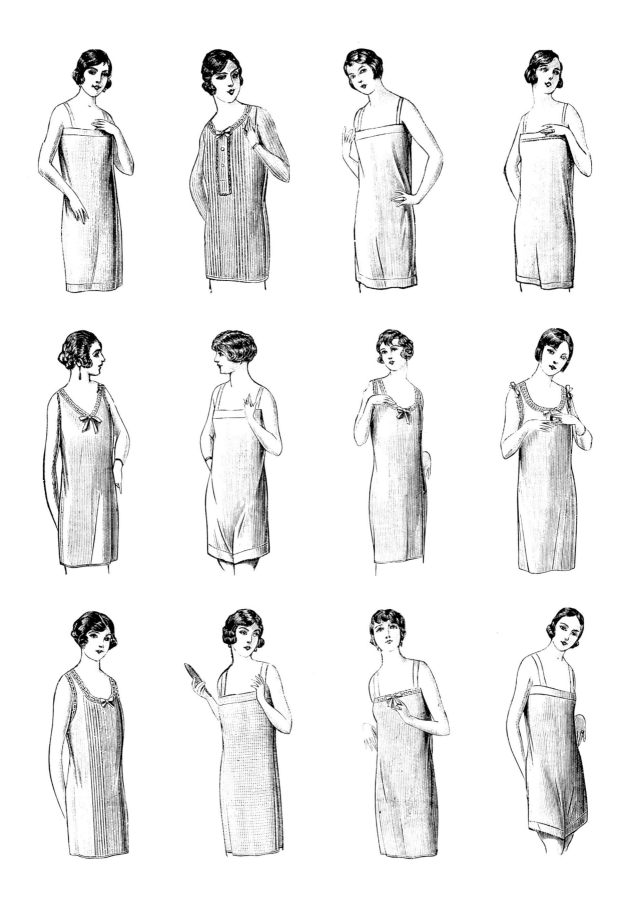

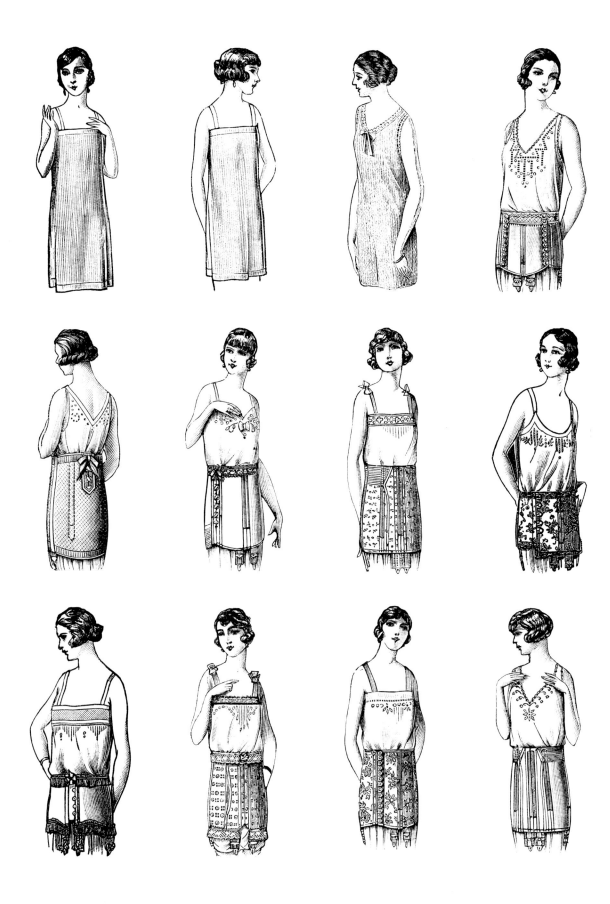

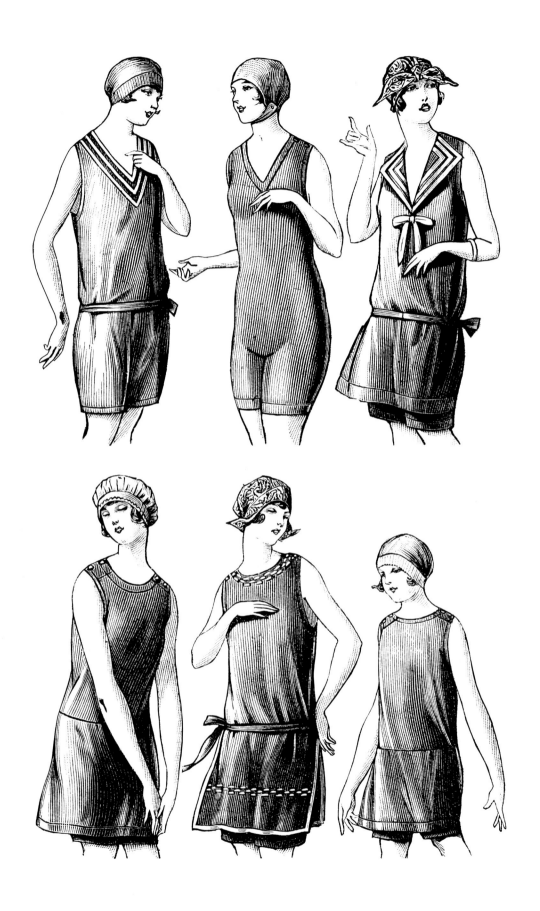

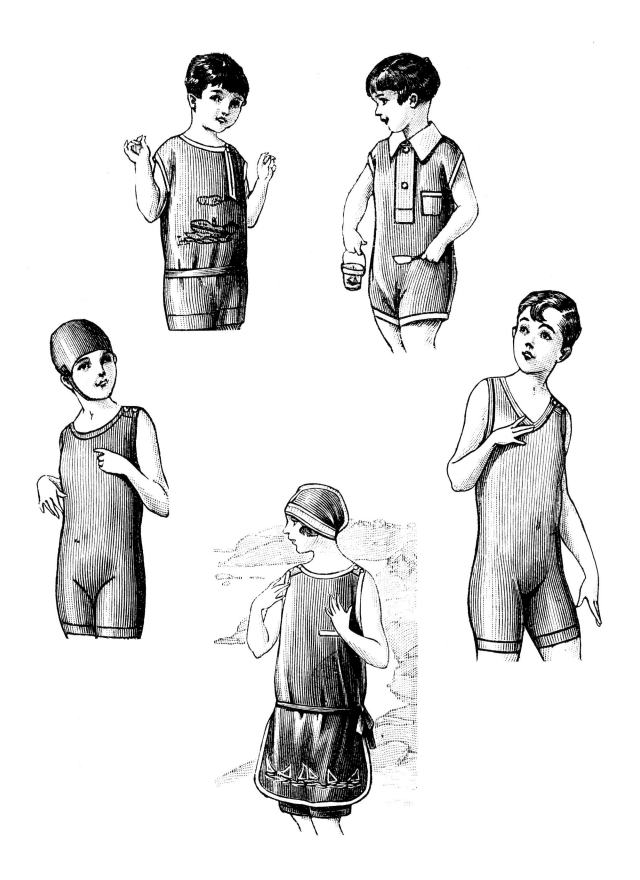

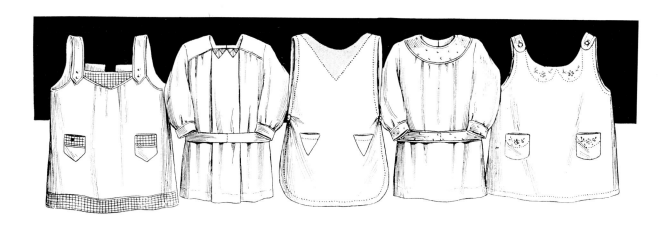

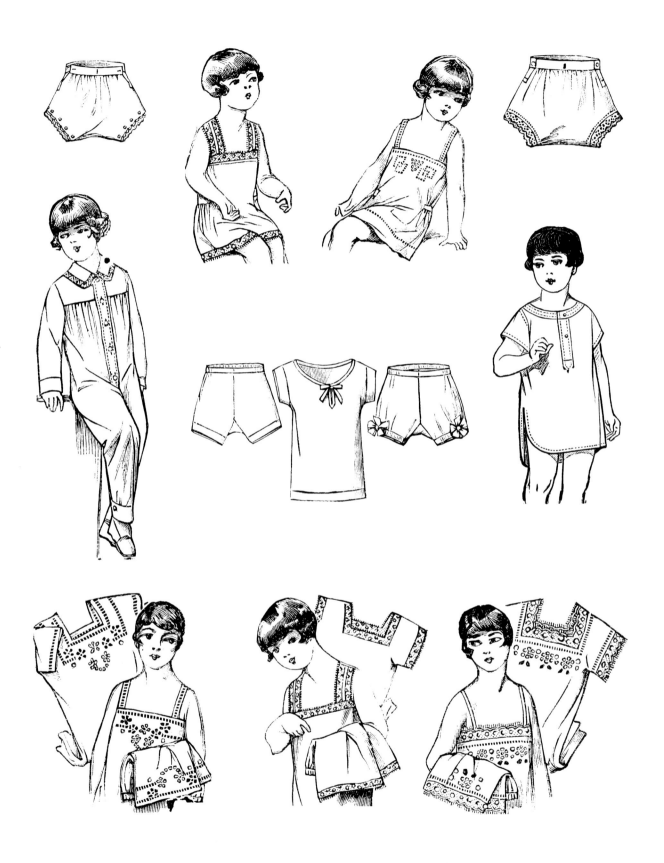

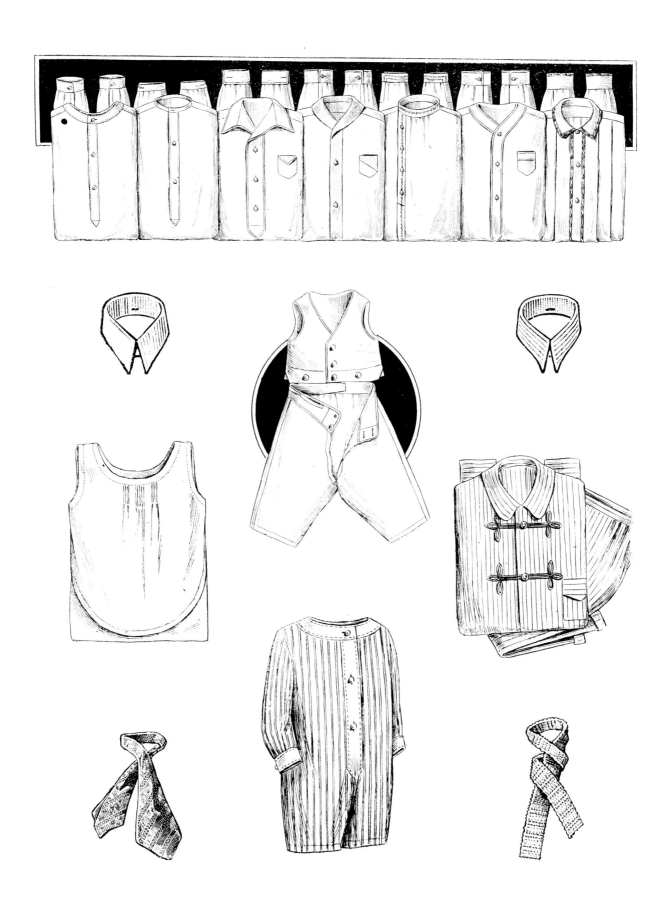

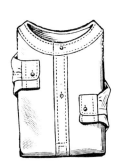

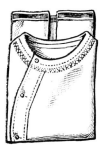

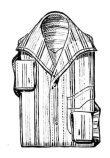

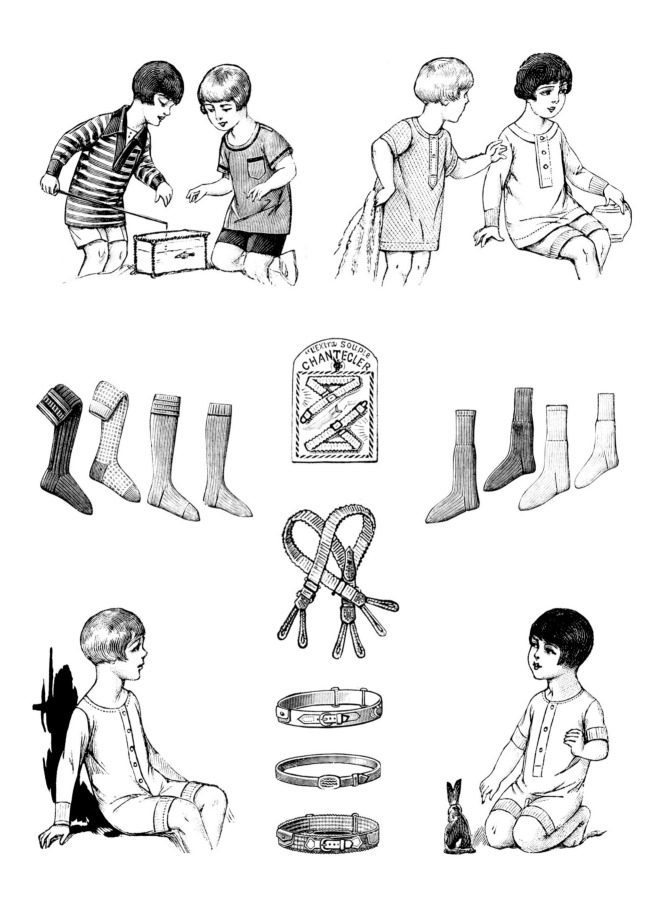

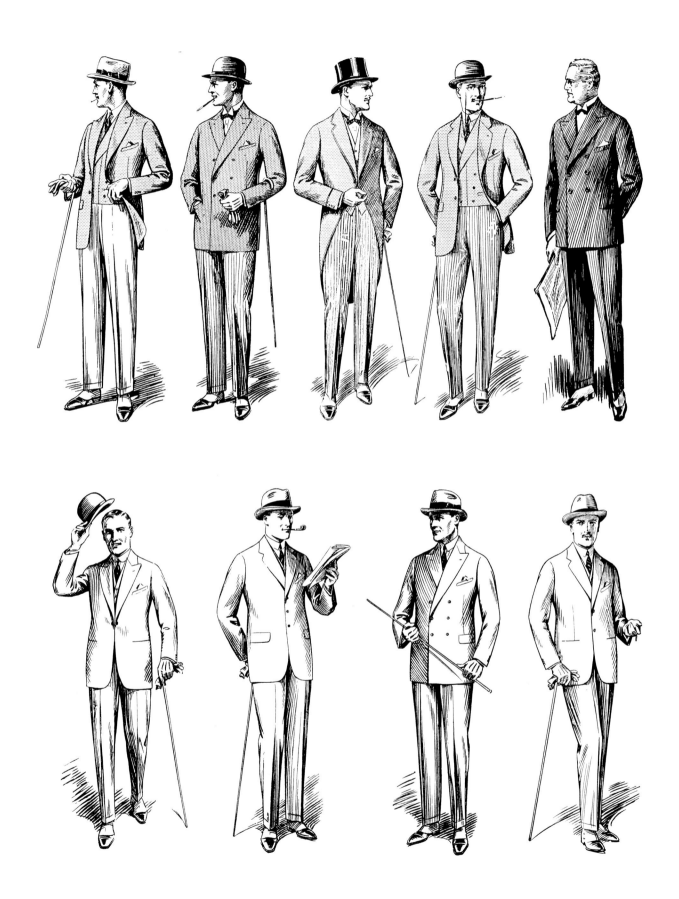

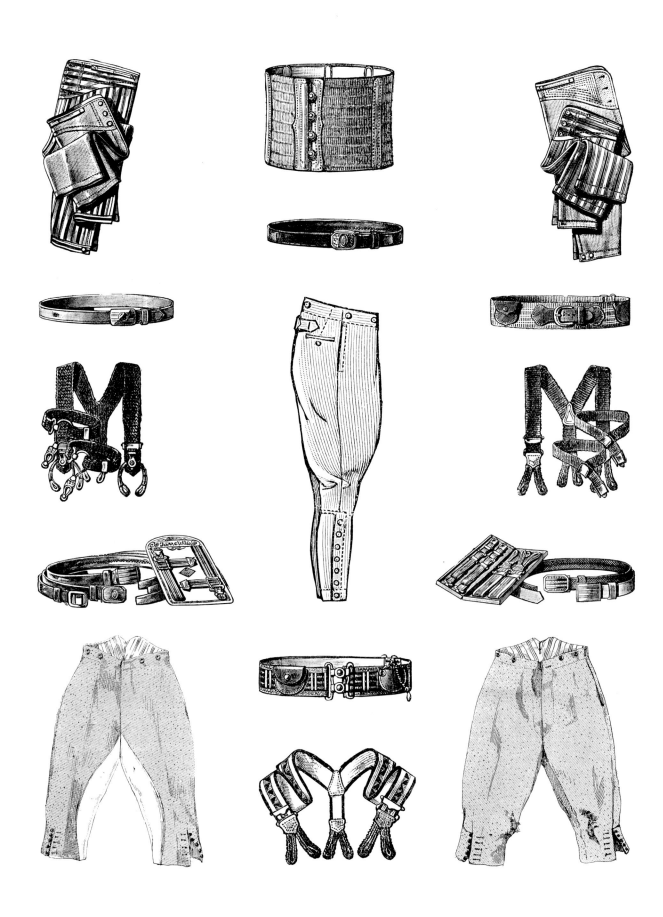

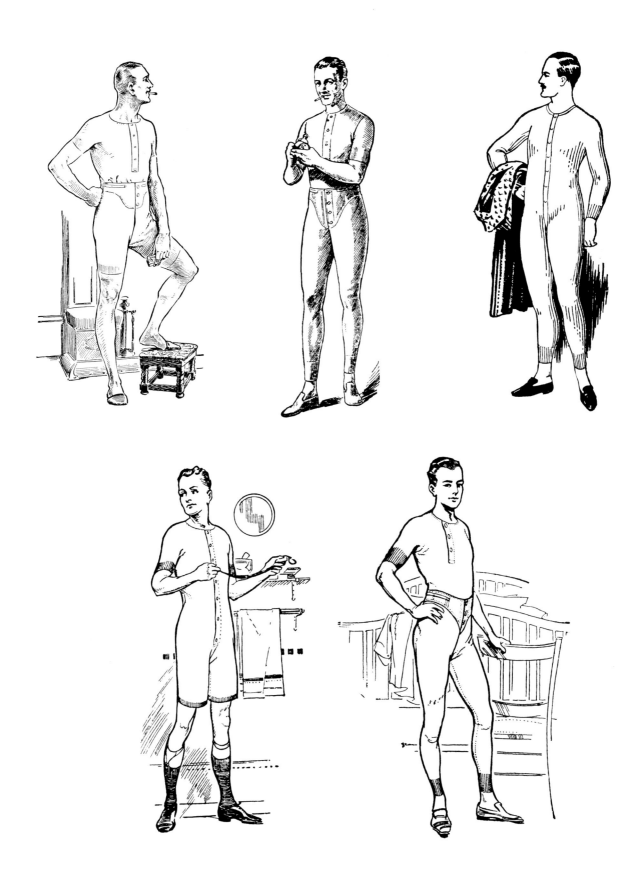

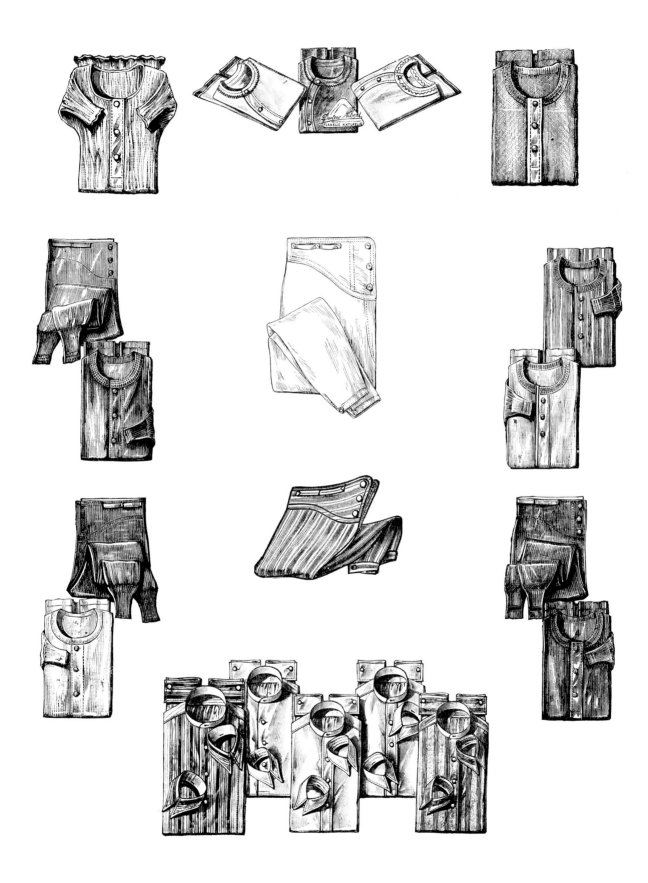

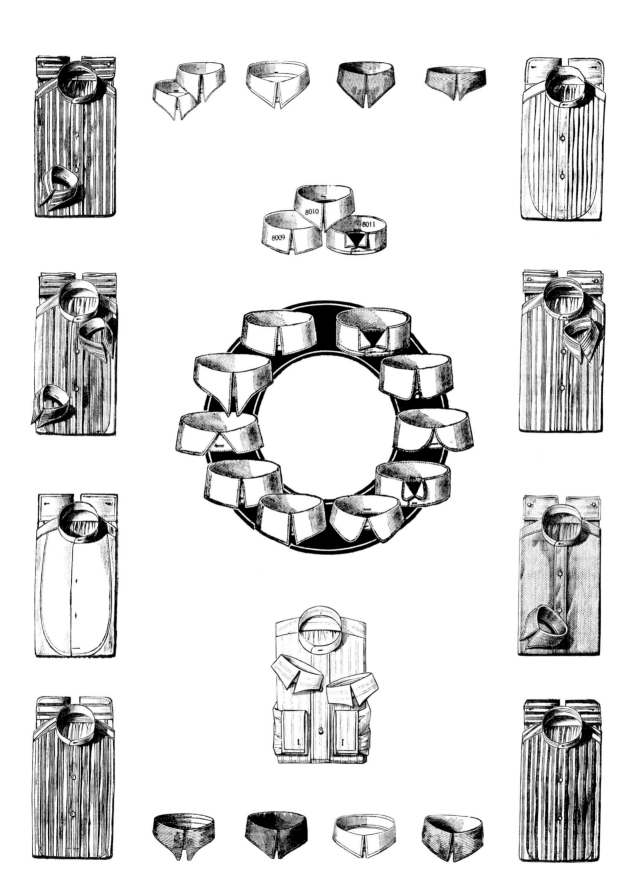

8010
8009
8011

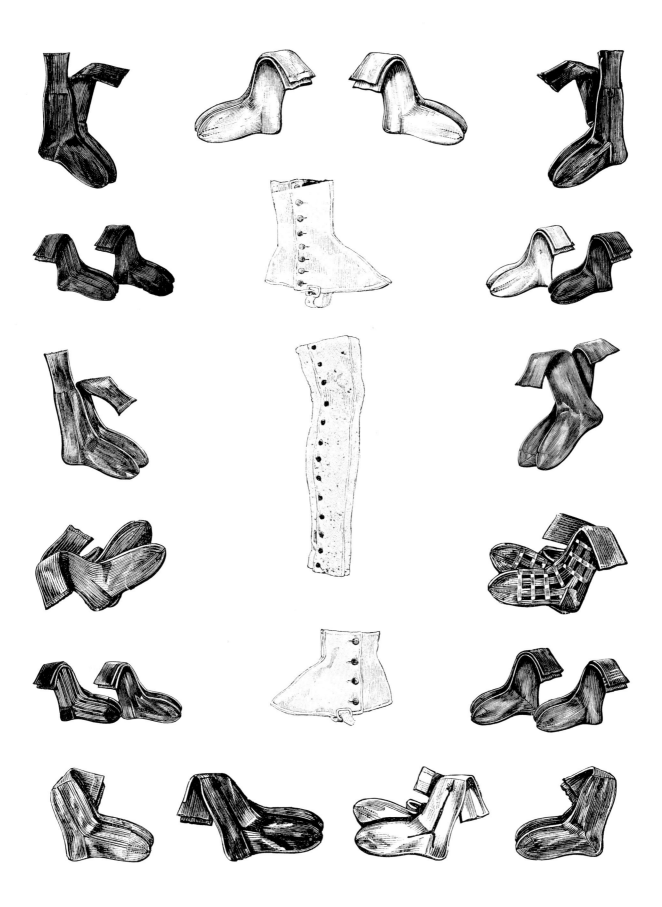